# Elephants Are Not Birds

BRAVE BOOKS

# Home of the Brave

Welcome to **Freedom Island**, Home of the Brave, where good battles evil and truth prevails. It's up to you to defend our great nation. Save the animals of Toke-A-Toke by completing the BRAVE Challenge at the end of this book.

Watch this video for an introduction to the story and BRAVE universe!

---

Saga One: The Origins

Book 1

**Elephants Are Not Birds**

Saga One: The Origins—Book 1

**Elephants Are Not Birds**

Copyright © 2021 by BRAVE BOOKS
All Rights Reserved

Book Illustrations © 2021 by Steliyana Doneva
Map Illustration © 2021 by Ali Elzeiny

Published by BRAVE BOOKS
www.BRAVEbooks.us

ISBN: 978-1-955550-49-9 (paperback)

First edition published in the USA in 2021 by BRAVE BOOKS

Now printed in the USA

All Rights Reserved. By purchase of this book, you have been licensed one copy for personal use only. No part of this work may be reproduced, redistributed, or used in any form or by any means without prior written permission of the publisher and copyright owner.

# Elephants Are Not Birds

Ashley St. Clair and BRAVE BOOKS
Art by Steliyana Doneva

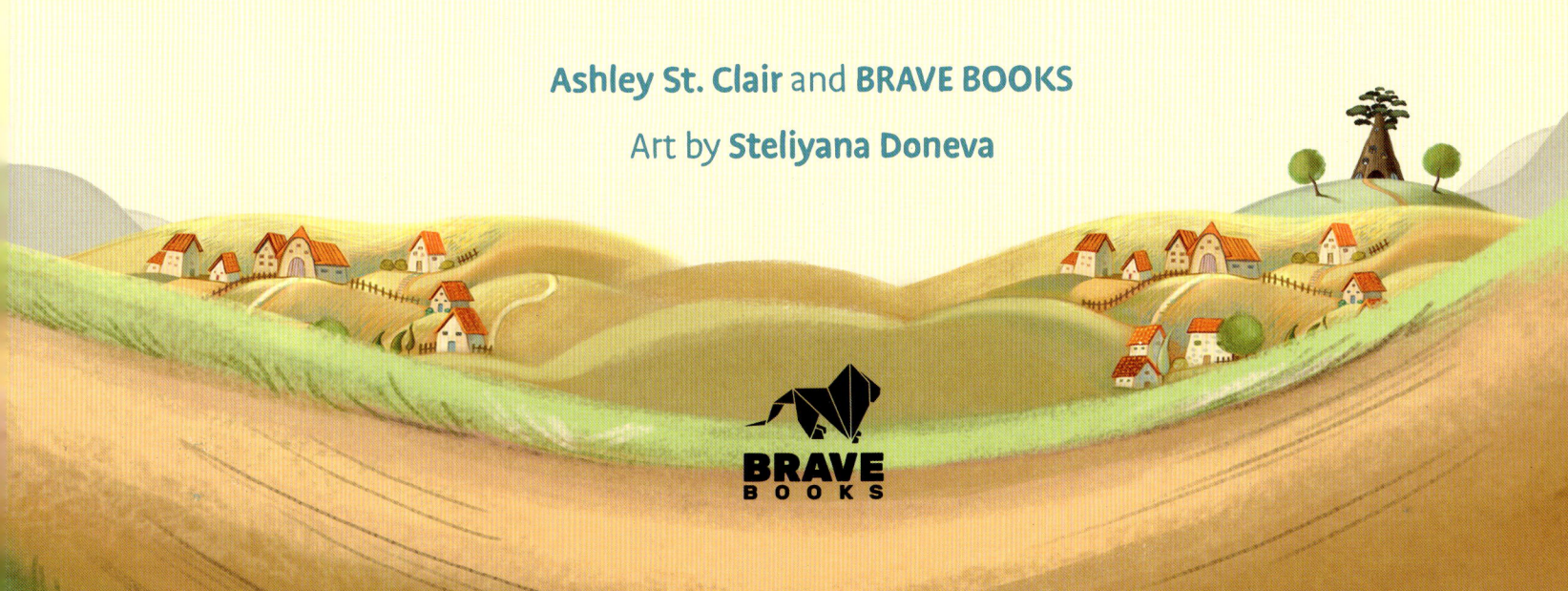

BRAVE BOOKS

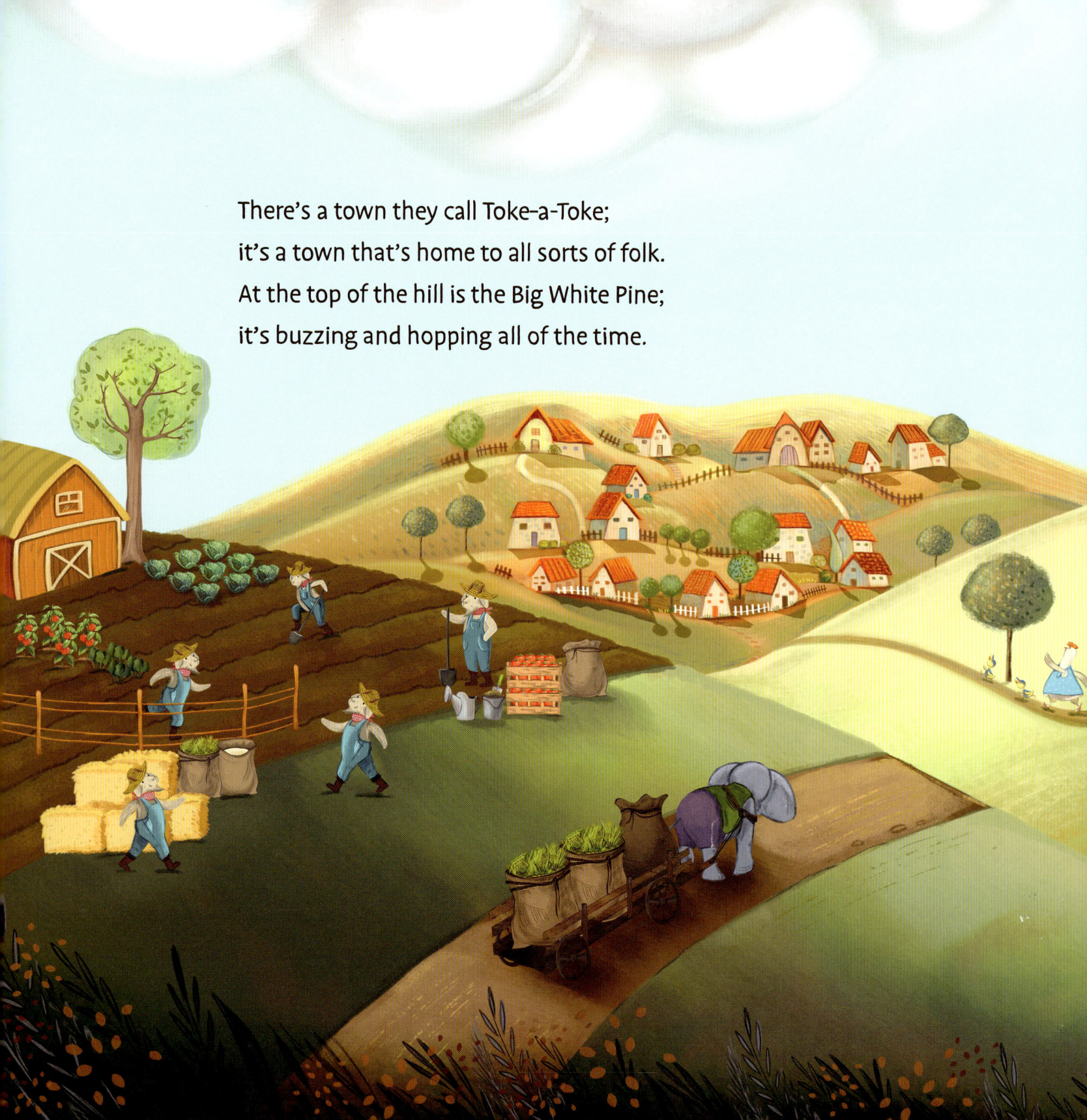

There's a town they call Toke-a-Toke;
it's a town that's home to all sorts of folk.
At the top of the hill is the Big White Pine;
it's buzzing and hopping all of the time.

To most of the animals, Toke-a-Toke felt like heaven,
but not to one elephant, whose name was Kevin.
Most elephants loved it when the clock hit noon,
but to Kevin, noon came far too soon.

That's when elephants pull carts up and down,
delivering supplies all over town.
"I don't mind the carrying or the bringing;
but, personally, I prefer to be singing."

A vulture named Culture was seeing and stalking,
until, with a grin, he started his squawking.

"My oh my, what a lovely sound!
Why are you carrying these carts around?
Your singing is the best I've heard.
Surely, oh surely, you must be a bird!"

# HA HA HA

"That's so very funny!
I'm as much a bird as you are a bunny."

"You laugh," said Culture, "but what would you rather—
sing songs or carry carts of food that's been gathered?"

"Hmm, it is true that I really love to sing.
Maybe being a bird is actually my thing."

"That's right," Culture squawked, "It's whatever you feel.
It's only your feelings that show what is real."

"Now is the time, let your bird life commence!
It's the only thing that seems to make sense."

"Here's what you need: a beak and some wings.
Take them—a bird needs these things."

"With my wings in their place, I begin a new day.
With beauty and grace, I sing on my way.
I'm now a fine birdy; so where do I start?
I guess I'll eat seeds; that feels right in my heart."

Kevin tried to peck a seed,
but his beak wouldn't grip.
"Maybe seeds aren't a need,
so that part I'll skip."

He tried building a nest,
but his twigs wouldn't stay.
He had failed this new test.
"Who needs nests anyway?"

"Being a bird is tough; I thought it'd be easy.
It's rougher than rough; frankly not breezy."

"There's one more thing to test if it's true:
I'll jump and then fly, like most birdies do."

Big Bear, though busy with baking and brewing, was totally baffled. "What's Kevin doing?"

Kevin was climbing the Big White Pine, gripping each branch, "I know I'll be fine!"
Step-by-step seeking to reach the high summit,
"Because I have wings, I know I won't plummet!"

BUT THEN...

Kevin slumped down, feeling upset.
His head hung low, as low as could get.

While Kevin was sulking he smelled something smoking.
The Big White Pine with fire was choking.

"We need a strong animal to lift heavy weight. Someone gray with stout legs and a trunk would be great."

Then, in the window, Kevin saw his reflection and noticed his size and big gray complexion.

"Silly me, the beak stops the use of my trunk.
The right choice I see is to get rid of this junk."
Kevin took action—his town was in peril!
So he sprayed water from a water-filled barrel.

# WHEW!

The fire's put out. Hooray, hooray!
It was Kevin the ELEPHANT who saved the day.

"Thank you! Oh, thank you!" the grateful bear said.
"If it weren't for you, we'd all be dead!"

THANK YOU!

HOORAY!

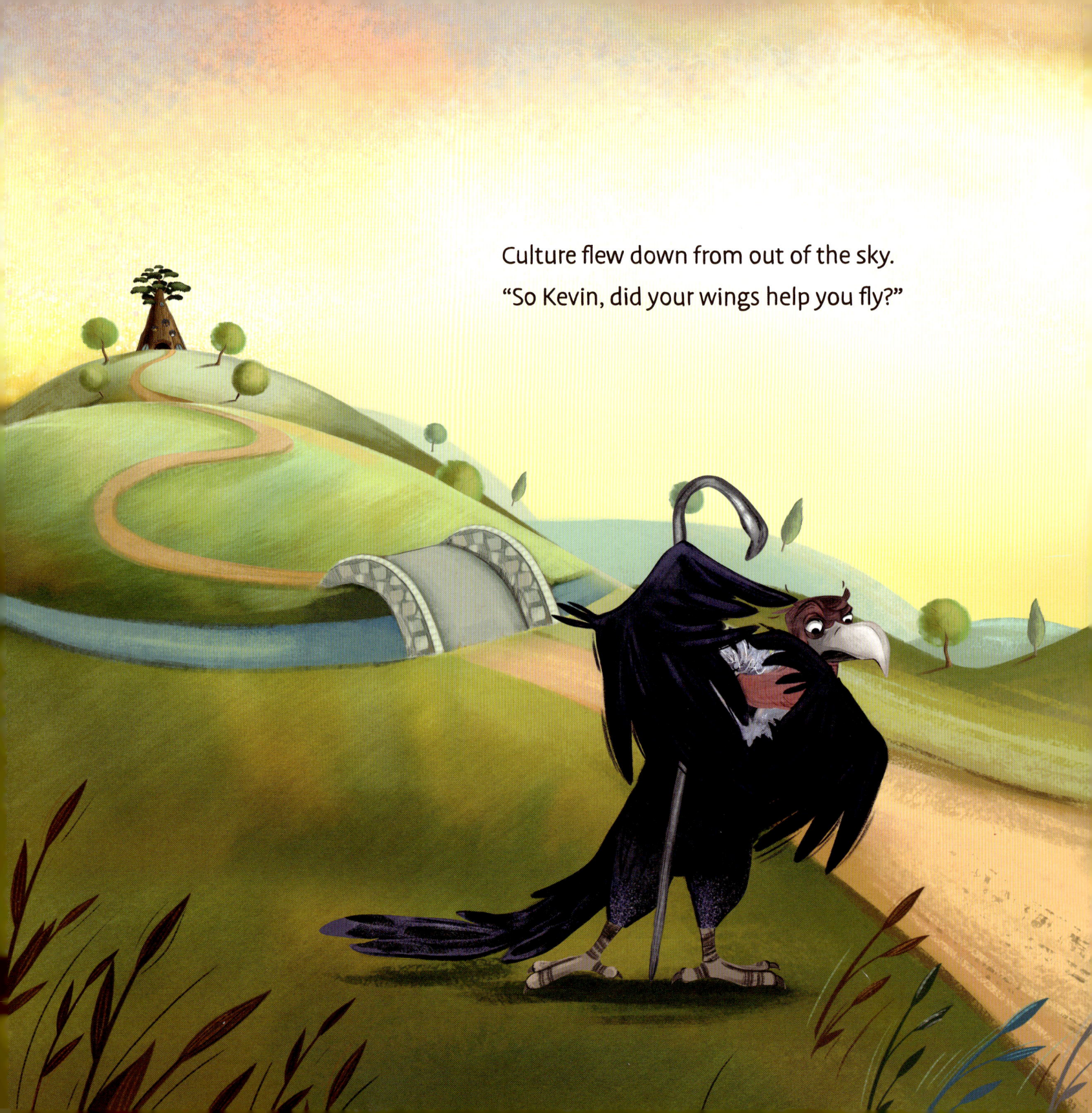

Culture flew down from out of the sky.

"So Kevin, did your wings help you fly?"

"Zip it, Culture! I'm not listening to you!
I am most free when I trust what is true.
I am an ELEPHANT; that's plain to see.
From this point on, I'll enjoy being me."

"I was right from the first. Tricky Culture was funny;
I'm no more a bird than he is a bunny."

"My life is not just about how I feel;
I can sing as an ELEPHANT; that's what is real!"

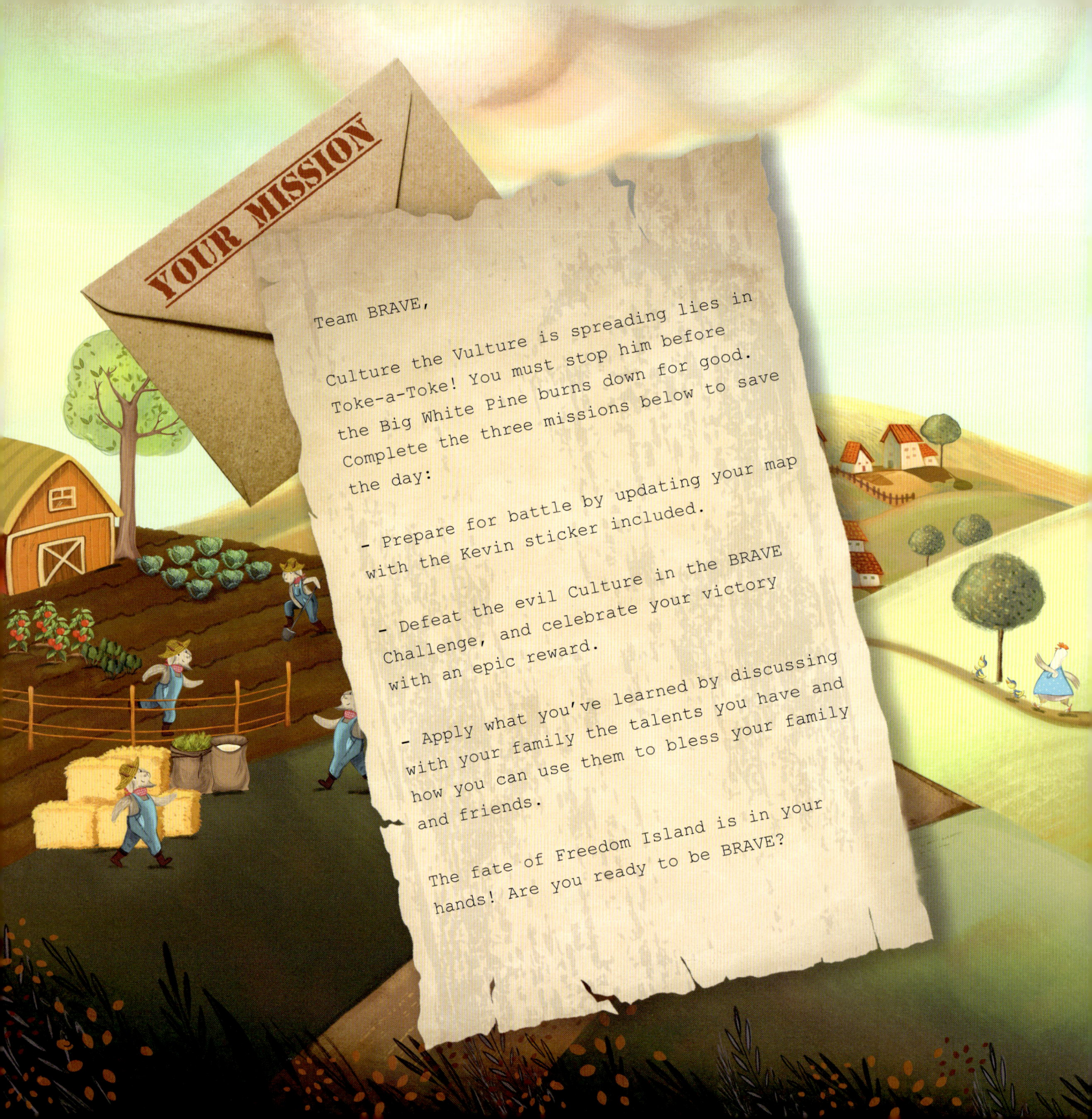

**YOUR MISSION**

Team BRAVE,

Culture the Vulture is spreading lies in Toke-a-Toke! You must stop him before the Big White Pine burns down for good. Complete the three missions below to save the day:

— Prepare for battle by updating your map with the Kevin sticker included.

— Defeat the evil Culture in the BRAVE Challenge, and celebrate your victory with an epic reward.

— Apply what you've learned by discussing with your family the talents you have and how you can use them to bless your family and friends.

The fate of Freedom Island is in your hands! Are you ready to be BRAVE?

## TO YOUR FAMILY

### INTRODUCTION

BRAVE Books has created the BRAVE Challenge to drive home key lessons and values illustrated in the story. Each activity (a game and the accompanying discussion questions) takes between 10 and 20 minutes. Family-focused and collaborative, the BRAVE Challenge is a quick and fun option for family game night.

The BRAVE Challenge works best with two or more BRAVE members, but it can be adapted for just one. To play with just one child and one parent, look for the "One Child Modification" icon.

### BRAVE CHALLENGE KEY

 Read aloud to the children

 One child modification

 Parents only

 Roll the die for Culture

## THE BRAVE CHALLENGE

### OBJECTIVE

Welcome to Team BRAVE! Your mission for this BRAVE Challenge is to defend Toke-A-Toke from Culture the Vulture. To get started, grab a sheet of paper and a pencil, and draw a scoreboard titled Team BRAVE vs. Culture, like the one shown.

| Culture | Team BRAVE |
|---------|------------|
| \|\|\|  | ⊮ \|\|     |

*While the children are creating the scoreboard, think about what they win if they defeat Culture. Here are a few ideas:*

- *Night out with parents*
- *Movie night*
- *Play the children's favorite game*
- *Putt-Putt golf*
- *Baking (and eating!) treats*
- *Bike ride*
- *Whatever gets your kiddos excited!*

## HOW TO PLAY

In this BRAVE Challenge, Team BRAVE (the children) will compete against Culture to earn points. At the end of all three activities, the team with the most points wins.

During each game the parent will roll a die for Culture. The number rolled will represent the number of points he earned in that game. Write this value on Culture's half of the scoreboard.

As you follow the instructions, Team BRAVE will also earn points. At the end of each game, we will write that value on the scoreboard under "Team BRAVE."

## WINNING

At the end, if Team BRAVE has earned more points than Culture then they have successfully defended Toke-A-Toke. The prize for winning will be _____. Let's begin!

## INTRODUCING...
## ASHLEY ST. CLAIR

Ashley St. Clair is a popular conservative influencer who has spent her career bringing awareness to issues close to her heart including free speech and gender identity. She helped BRAVE Books write this story and the BRAVE Challenge. She will be popping in to give you ideas on how you can explain these concepts to your child.

### ASHLEY SUGGESTS

"Have fun! Your children should love this, but it will make the whole experience even better for them if you get into it and have fun with them, too!"

## GAME #1 – VOICE OF TRUTH

### LESSON
Discerning truth from confusion.

### MATERIALS NEEDED
A six-sided die and a blindfold.

### OBJECTIVE

Culture the Vulture is trying to trick the members of Team BRAVE! You will guide your blindfolded teammate through Toke-A-Toke and ignore Culture so that your teammate doesn't wander off and get lost.

# INSTRUCTIONS

 *Roll the die, and **record Culture's score on the scoreboard.***

1. Blindfold one member of Team BRAVE.
2. A parent will set up obstacles throughout the room.
3. The blindfolded team member will start with six points at one end of the room and begin moving to the other side.
4. Team BRAVE loses one point for every object the blindfolded member bumps.
5. The rest of the team will shout encouragement and advice to guide their teammate to safety using words only—they cannot guide the team member with touch.
6. A parent acting as Culture will try to confuse and distract the BRAVE member from reaching the next room by giving bad advice and instructions.
7. Repeat with each BRAVE member.
8. Average the BRAVE members' points to find Team BRAVE's score, and **record this number on the scoreboard.**

 ## ONE CHILD MODIFICATION

If only one child and one parent are playing, have the parent give both good and bad advice, altering his or her voice to indicate whether she is speaking for Culture or a BRAVE team member.

Game on!

 # TALK ABOUT IT

1. How did it feel when you couldn't see and didn't know where to go?
2. How did it feel knowing there was a voice trying to trick you?
3. In our story, Kevin trusted Culture. What happened when you trusted Culture's voice in today's game?

4. Where are some places you might hear things that aren't true?

### ASHLEY SUGGESTS

"Help your children realize there are certain places where there are potentially harmful voices (for example, school or the playground)."

5. How did it feel to know there were voices you could trust? How did you focus on the truth instead of listening to the voice that was trying to confuse you?
6. Where can you hear things that you know are true? Why?

### ASHLEY SUGGESTS

"Your children can trust you, the parent, because you love them and know what's best for them. They can also trust solid science, the facts that we have observed to be consistently true about the world."

7. What should you do when you hear something you aren't sure is true?
8. Why is choosing true voices to listen to in real life even more important than in this game?
9. Are you a trustworthy voice? Can your siblings and parents trust you? Why?

## GAME #2 - SCAVENGER HUNT

### LESSON
Changing something's appearance cannot change its identity.

### MATERIALS NEEDED
A six-sided die, paper and crayons, and a timer or stopwatch.

Video Tutorial

 ## OBJECTIVE

Culture has tricked Kevin's friends into thinking that they are something they're not! Look around Toke-A-Toke (your house) for these friends, and fight Culture's lies with the truth. Hurry! You have two minutes to complete your mission.

 ## INSTRUCTIONS

 *Roll the die, and **record Culture's score on the scoreboard.***

1. Each member of Team BRAVE has three minutes to make three drawings on separate pages, have one drawing of a horse, one of a man, and one of a dog.
2. When team BRAVE is finished, they will go to a bedroom so that a parent can hide the drawings around the house, as directed below.
3. The parent will give Team BRAVE three clues and start a timer for two minutes.
4. Team BRAVE earns six points for finding all three drawings in under two minutes; four points for finding two of the drawings; two points for one drawing; and no points if they find none. **Record Team BRAVE's points on the scoreboard.**

*A parent will hide the man drawing in a freezer, the dog drawing on top of the stove, and the horse drawing on some shoes.*

 *The clues are: Culture has tried to turn the men into "cool dudes," the dogs into "hot dogs," and the horses into "horseshoes."*

*If your children are struggling to find the drawings, feel free to give them extra hints!*

*Are you ready? Game on!*

 ## TALK ABOUT IT

1. Did Culture really change the man into a cool dude, the dog into a hot dog, and the horse into a horseshoe?

2. Can we change something to another thing by changing its appearance or location? Why or why not? What about if we changed its features like putting ketchup on the dog?

### ASHLEY SUGGESTS

"You want your children to recognize that things have an inherent nature that doesn't change."

3. Kevin the Elephant tried to make himself a bird by strapping wings to his back. How much did that make him a bird? Why can't an elephant fly?
4. For the boys, ask "If you put on some of mommy's lipstick, would you turn into a girl?" For the girls, ask, "If you shaved off shaving cream from your face would you turn into a man?" Why?

### ASHLEY SUGGESTS

"Help your kids realize that our gender is part of the way God made us. He put it in our DNA, and we can't change that."

5. What is super cool about being a girl? What is super cool about being a boy? What are some supercool elements boys and girls share? What are some things boys and girls don't share? Why is this good?
6. Why are you happy to be the gender that you are?

### ASHLEY SUGGESTS

"Be sure that you answer this question too! Tell your kids why you like being the gender you are and especially why you liked it at their age. You are a significant gender model for your children."

45

## GAME #3 - ALL MIXED UP

### LESSON
All things have a purpose.

### MATERIALS NEEDED
A six-sided die, paper and crayons, a blindfold, a plush ball, and a timer or stopwatch.

### OBJECTIVE

Toke-A-Toke has nearly been saved from Culture. We just need you to help with a few small tasks before we can have victory over this mean vulture. Complete the six mini-games, worth one point each.

### INSTRUCTIONS

Roll the die, and **record Culture's score on the scoreboard.**

**Mini-Game 1:** Pick one player from Team BRAVE. A parent will whisper a secret word to the player, who will hold his or her tongue with his fingers and repeat the word to the rest of Team BRAVE. If Team BRAVE can guess the word in 30 seconds or less, they win a point.

*The word is "squirrel."*

### ONE CHILD MODIFICATION

A parent holds his own tongue and says squirrel for the child to guess.

**Mini-Game 2:** Pick another member of Team BRAVE to draw a picture using only his feet. A parent will whisper a prompt to the BRAVE member. If the rest of Team BRAVE can guess what he is drawing in one minute or less, Team BRAVE scores a point.

*The picture prompt is "Kevin the Elephant."*

**ONE CHILD MODIFICATION**

Have the child draw a picture of any character in the book, and let the parent guess who it is.

**Mini-Game 3**: Blindfold a member of Team BRAVE, and have her touch someone else's face. If she can guess the face she is touching in 10 seconds or less, Team BRAVE scores a point.

 **ONE CHILD MODIFICATION**

Have the blindfolded child touch an object in the room instead of a face.

**Mini-Game 4:** Choose two members of Team BRAVE to make a human wheelbarrow. If they can walk 10 feet in one minute, Team BRAVE wins one point.

 **ONE CHILD MODIFICATION**

Have the BRAVE member try to walk three steps on his hands without letting his feet touch the ground.

**Mini-Game 5:** Choose a member of Team BRAVE to use only her knees to catch a plush ball. A parent will toss the ball five times to give her five chances. If she catches it, Team BRAVE scores a point.

**Mini-Game 6:** Choose two members of Team BRAVE to use their elbows as hands and pass a ball back and forth. If they can pass the ball 10 times in 30 seconds or less without dropping it, Team BRAVE wins one point.

 **ONE CHILD MODIFICATION**

Have the BRAVE member try to put ten balls into a basket or onto a table in thirty seconds.

*Blindfold your child and hand him or her an object to guess what it is.*

 ## TALK ABOUT IT

1. Why do you think God gave you a tongue? Feet? Hands? What are at least two purposes for each?
2. How can you use each of those body parts for good? What about for bad?
3. What was Kevin the Elephant's purpose at the end of the book? How did he discover that purpose? How did Kevin help others by living according to his purpose?
4. What are some things you are good at? How can you use those to help your family and others?

 ### ASHLEY SUGGESTS

"Encourage the children to bring up qualities or skills that their siblings have."

## TALLY ALL THE POINTS TO SEE WHO WON!

### BRAVE SUMMARY

Though Kevin the Elephant loved to sing, he quickly realized that he was not a bird, no matter what Culture the Vulture said. Your gender is a part of who you are, and you were made this way for a specific purpose. Your purpose does not change just because other people say so. Boys are boys, and girls are girls. Who you are is wonderful and special—it's worth celebrating!